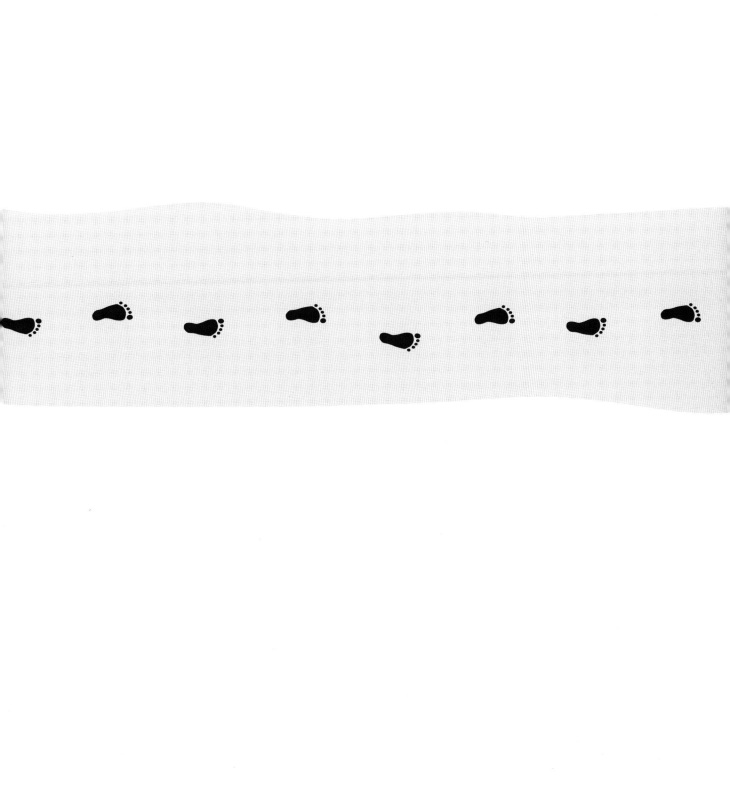

Published by

Gospel Standard Trust Publications
12(b) Roundwood Lane, Harpenden,
Herts, AL5 3BZ, UK
www.gospelstandard.org.uk

ISBN 9781897837658

Managed and Manufactured by: Jellyfish Solutions Ltd.

faithful footsteps

Elijah
Prophet of God

B A Ramsbottom

Illustrated by
M H Philpott

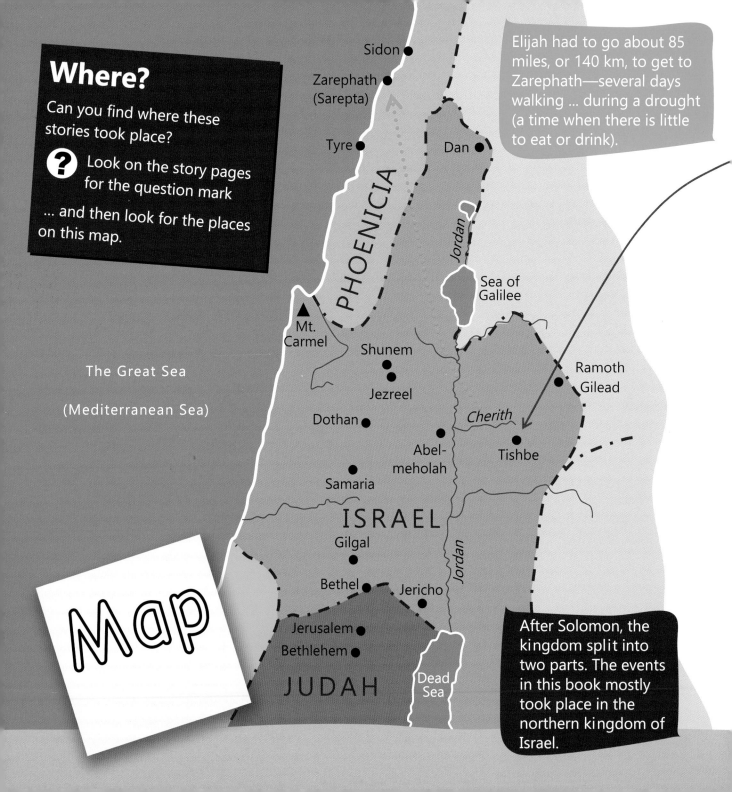

Where?

Can you find where these stories took place?

? Look on the story pages for the question mark

... and then look for the places on this map.

Elijah had to go about 85 miles, or 140 km, to get to Zarephath—several days walking ... during a drought (a time when there is little to eat or drink).

After Solomon, the kingdom split into two parts. The events in this book mostly took place in the northern kingdom of Israel.

Sidon

Zarephath (Sarepta)

Tyre

Dan

PHOENICIA

Jordan

Sea of Galilee

Mt. Carmel

Shunem

Jezreel

Ramoth Gilead

The Great Sea

(Mediterranean Sea)

Dothan

Cherith

Abel-meholah

Tishbe

Samaria

ISRAEL

Gilgal

Jordan

Bethel

Jericho

Jerusalem

Bethlehem

Dead Sea

JUDAH

Map

Who was Elijah?

Elijah came from a small place called Tishbe in a part of Israel called Gilead. This is why he is called 'Elijah the Tishbite.'

He was a prophet. A prophet is someone who God used in Bible times to tell people what God wanted them to know. Today God doesn't send prophets because he speaks to us through the Bible, the Word of God.

DID YOU KNOW?
Elijah means 'My God is the LORD'

DID YOU KNOW?
In the New Testament, Elijah is called Elias

The Lord Jesus and Elijah

Jesus talked about Elijah going to stay with a widow woman (Luke 4) and also said John the Baptist was like Elijah (Matthew 17).

Who was Ahab?

Ahab was a king in Israel. He was married to a woman named Jezebel. They were both wicked people who worshipped a false god called Baal.

These stories happened here

History Timeline

| Adam, Noah, Babel | Abraham, Moses, Joshua | Judges, David Solomon | Kings of Israel and Judah | Daniel, Esther, Nehemiah | The Lord Jesus Christ |

Elijah and the Ravens

What are those fierce black birds? And what are they doing? They are ravens. They are carrying something in their mouths—bread, meat—but they are not eating it. Where are they taking it?

There all alone by a little brook of water called Cherith is a hairy, rough looking man. His name is Elijah. He is a prophet of God. He has just been to the wicked King Ahab and told him that because all the people are so evil, God will punish them. For three years it will not rain. It is terrible when there is no rain—nothing growing, everything dying, nothing to eat or drink.

? *On the map, can you find:* **CHERITH**

But what about the poor prophet? Why is he by the little brook? God has told him to be there. Even if no one else has anything to drink, Elijah has.

This brook has not dried up. Elijah can drink the water there and it is God who has sent the fierce black birds carrying food for him to eat.

God has promised He will always supply His people's needs. He still does today. Morning after morning and evening after evening, the ravens never failed to come.

DID YOU KNOW? A brook is a small stream

So Elijah was not left hungry and thirsty. Wouldn't it have been lovely to hear him when he thanked God?

You can read about this in the first Book of Kings, chapter 17, verses 1 to 7.

Elijah and the Widow Woman

We wonder what Elijah is thinking? The brook is drying up.
What will happen when there is no water left in it?
What must he do? God has not told him.

At last the little brook did dry up and now God tells
Elijah what to do. He must go a long way, to another
country, and a poor widow woman will look after him.
But a poor widow? How could she even look after herself?

Anyway, Elijah set off. At last he reaches the place. It was called
Zarephath and what do you think is the first thing that he sees?
The poor widow. She is gathering a few sticks to make a fire, make
something to eat for herself and her little boy—and then they would
have nothing left. It seemed worse than the Brook Cherith.

But Elijah called out, "Bring me a drink of water," and, "Fetch me a
piece of bread." He was sure that God would look after them! And He
did. All the time Elijah lived with the widow woman, there was always

? *On the map, can you find:* **ZAREPHATH**

some meal and some oil left to make something to eat. They never starved. Elijah knew that "the Lord will provide." He has said so, and what God says is always true.

You can read about this in the first Book of Kings, chapter 17, verses 8 to 16.

Elijah and the Little Boy

Something terrible has happened. The widow woman's little boy has died. His poor mother is very sad.

What could Elijah do? He knew that God can do anything. He knew that even now God could bring him back to life. So he picked the little boy up and carried him up into the little room where he slept. There he laid him on his bed, stretched himself on him, and prayed to his God. The little boy began to move. He was alive. God had performed a miracle. He had answered Elijah's prayers.

DID YOU KNOW?
This boy was the first person that God brought back to life

So now Elijah picked him up, brought him downstairs, and gave him to his mother. Wouldn't she be glad to see him alive again?

"Ah!" she said to Elijah, "now I do know that you are a man of God and God's words you speak are truth." And that is just what Elijah the prophet was—a man of God.

You can read about this in the first Book of Kings, chapter 17, verses 17 to 24.

Elijah and the Wicked Prophets

A long time had passed and God spoke to Elijah again. "Go to the wicked king Ahab and tell him it is going to rain."

We wonder if Elijah was frightened. Would the king kill him? But he must have been sad, too, to leave the widow woman who had been so kind to him, and the little boy. But he went.

What he saw was terrible. No rain for so long—nothing growing, streams dried up, not enough grass for the horses and cows. It was because God was angry with His people Israel.

When Elijah met the king, the king was furious. He blamed Elijah for it all. "No," said Elijah, "it is because you and the people are so bad. You have left the true God and are worshipping a false God." (He was called Baal.)

But Elijah was not frightened. Do you know what he did? He told the king what to do! And the king did it. God was with Elijah. "Get all the false prophets of Baal together on the big mountain called Carmel," said Elijah. There were hundreds of them. Elijah told all the people he was going to ask God to show them who was right. Was it he or all these others? God or Baal?

How would he do it? Both sides were to have a bullock. They both would cut their bullock in pieces, put wood under it, and then cry to God to send down fire from heaven and burn it up.

Baal's prophets tried first. They cried for hours. "Baal, hear us." But nothing happened. Elijah laughed at them. "Perhaps Baal is asleep. Wake him up. Shout louder!" Still nothing happened. The wicked prophets of Baal even cut themselves with knives—as if this would make Baal hear.

Then Elijah came forward. He called all the people to watch.
But whatever is he doing? Pouring water all over his bullock.

? *On the map, can you find:* **MT. CARMEL**

It seemed a silly thing to do, but Elijah wanted to make it really hard for it to be burned up.

Then he prayed. He called on the true God. And see what is happening—fire coming down from heaven, burning up the bullock, and even the water. God has spoken.

All the people cried, "The LORD He is the God. The LORD He is the God." And all the evil prophets of Baal were put to death.

But that is not the end.

You can read about this in the first Book of Kings, chapter 18, verses 17 to 40.

Rain from Heaven

Poor King Ahab must have been frightened. Would they kill him too? "Get on your way," said Elijah, "because it is going to rain hard soon." What a thing to say! It had not rained for over three years.

Then Elijah fell down before his God and prayed for the rain. But nothing happened. He sent his servant again and again, but he kept coming back and saying he could see nothing. But Elijah did not give up. "Go again!" and this time the servant said, "I can see a little cloud in the sky."

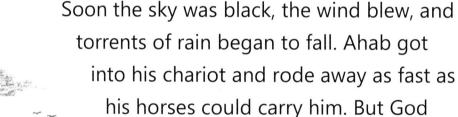

Soon the sky was black, the wind blew, and torrents of rain began to fall. Ahab got into his chariot and rode away as fast as his horses could carry him. But God gave Elijah such strength that he ran faster than the king's chariot.

The Bible tells us that Elijah was a man like ourselves. But he prayed, and it did not rain for three years; and then prayed again, and it did rain. Elijah's God is the God who hears and answers prayer.

You can read about this in the first Book of Kings, chapter 18, verses 41 to 46.

Running Away!

What is happening to Elijah now? He looks frightened, not happy like yesterday. He is running away.

The wicked king's wife Jezebel has said she is going to kill him because of what he has done. Her prophets have been killed, so now she is going to kill Elijah.

So he runs away. On and on and on he goes, right into a desert, and there he falls down under a tree and wants to die. He is weary and tired. He falls asleep.

But Elijah's God has not forgotten him. He sends an angel down from heaven, and that angel bakes a cake for him to eat. Then the angel wakes him up. He eats the cake and has a drink, and then falls asleep again.

Another time the angel wakes him, and tells him he has a long journey to go. This time it is something wonderful the angel gives him

to eat—because after this he can still go on day after day without eating anything else. God has been very kind to him.

At last Elijah comes to a cave and hides there—but he cannot hide from God, can he? "What are you doing here, Elijah?" God asks him. His God is still with him and tells him he has more work for him to do. He must go and find the man who is going to be his servant and friend. He is called Elisha, and he too will be a prophet of God.

So Elijah did what God told him and went back. Soon he sees a young man ploughing in a field. Yes, it is Elisha. So he threw his mantle, his cloak, over him.

And Elisha knew what it meant! So he leaves everything to go to be with his new master. Don't you think Elijah would now be glad after being sad for so long?

You can read about this in the first Book of Kings, chapter 19.

Naboth's Vineyard

We are back with the wicked King Ahab again. He never learns. He is as bad as ever.

There was a man whose name was Naboth. He had a lovely vineyard—a place where plants full of beautiful grapes grew. It was near where the king lived in Jezreel, and when he looked over from the palace, he thought, "I want it for myself."

But Naboth would not let the king have it. He knew God wanted him to keep it for himself. So what do you think the wicked queen did? She thought up an evil plan. She got lots of people to tell lies about Naboth and say he had done bad things. Then they had him killed, people throwing big stones at him.

King Ahab is happy. There he is, strutting down to this lovely vineyard he has now got for himself. But someone is waiting for him there. Yes, it is Elijah. Elijah told him he is going to die. God is going to punish him—and his evil wife Jezebel. Soon they would both be killed and it would be in a horrible way.

 On the map, can you find: **JEZREEL**

It all happened just as Elijah had said. God will always have the last word with people who sin against him.

You can read about this in the first Book of Kings, chapter 21.

DID YOU KNOW? When Jezebel died, she was not buried. She was eaten by dogs

Fire from Heaven Again

The king who followed Ahab was nearly as bad! His name was Ahaziah. But he was ill. He had fallen from an upstairs window and hurt himself badly. He wondered if he was going to die.

So he did a very wicked and foolish thing. He sent to the false god Baal to ask if he would get better again.

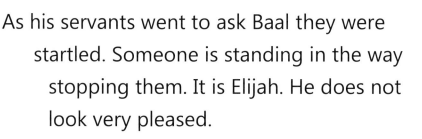

As his servants went to ask Baal they were startled. Someone is standing in the way stopping them. It is Elijah. He does not look very pleased.

"Why are you seeking Baal," he said, "when there is a God in heaven? But I can tell you what is going to happen. The king is going to die."

So the King's servants went back to him. King Ahaziah was angry when he heard the news. Why did he not say

he was sorry and pray to the true God in heaven? But no! He sends fifty soldiers to capture Elijah and bring him to him. There they found him, sitting on the top of a hill.

But God was with Elijah, and sent down fire from heaven and burned them all up.

But the wicked king tried the same thing again, and again the same thing happened. Another fifty soldiers sent to capture Elijah—more fire from heaven, and all of them burned up.

DID YOU KNOW?
Ahaziah was living in his palace in Samaria when he fell

You can hardly believe it. King Ahaziah tried again a third time. But this time the poor captain of the soldiers was frightened. He did not want to be burned to death. So he knelt down before Elijah and asked that his life might be spared. The captain did not have to capture him. Elijah let him take him back to the king. He was not frightened, for God was with him.

When Elijah met the king, he told him plainly the sad news. He would not get better. He would die. He should never have sent to Baal. He should have prayed to God.

❓ *On the map, can you find:* **SAMARIA**

So he died, just as God had said. What a sad end!

You can read about this in the second Book of Kings, chapter 1.

Elijah goes up to Heaven

Did you know that Elijah never died? He was carried up to heaven in a chariot of fire.

Now his work was ended. He had been a good servant of his God.

One day Elijah took his friend Elisha with him. They went from one place to another. Elijah kept saying, "Stop here. I will go on." But Elisha said, "No." He felt sure something was going to happen.

They came to the River Jordan, but how would they get across? Elijah took off his mantle, and struck the river, and the water stopped flowing so they could go across on dry ground.

DID YOU KNOW? The children of Israel also went across Jordan on dry ground

But now Elijah stopped and asked Elisha a question. What would he like his master to do for him? It was a big question. Elisha answered that he would like "more of Elijah's spirit." Elijah had a wonderful spirit: praying to God, trusting him, obeying him—because God was with his spirit.

This is what Elisha knew he badly needed as God's prophet, after Elijah had been taken up to heaven.

 On the map, can you find: the River **JORDAN** *(near Jericho)*

"If you see what happens, God will give it you," said Elijah. And while they were talking, a chariot of fire came down and carried him right up to heaven.

As he was being carried up, his mantle fell down. And Elisha *did* see it.

Poor Elisha must have felt very sad. He had lost his master and his friend. And God's people had lost their prophet and their leader. What would happen now?

Soon he knew the answer. He was back at the River Jordan. No way across! Elijah has gone. What about Elijah's God? Is He still with them? But Elisha had Elijah's mantle, and he knew what happened before. So, trusting in God, he took the mantle, struck the water just as his master had done, and the same thing happened again. God made a way over.

Yes, Elijah had gone to heaven, but God was still with Elisha, still with His people, and would still do wonderful things for them. He is the same God today.

DID YOU KNOW?
At least 50 other people saw Elijah go up to heaven

You can read about this in the second Book of Kings, chapter 2, verses 1 to 14.

Can you remember?

Look at this page to help you remember the story of Elijah.

If you have enjoyed this book, why not get a *Sketches...* colouring book?

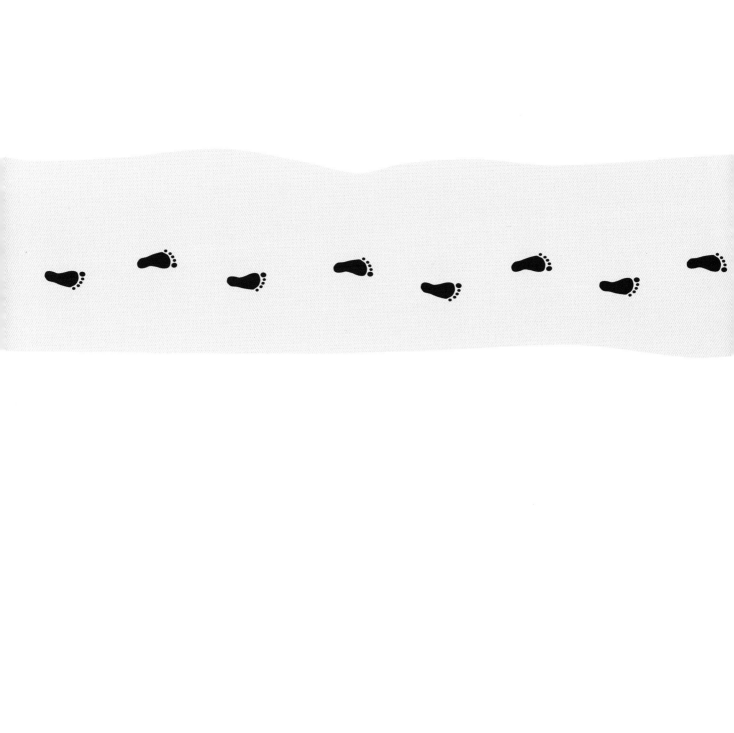